For more information about Cape Cod Eco-Tales, visit us online:
www.capecodecotales.com

Vernal Pool Visitors

by Heidi Clemmer
illustrated by Marisa Picariello

Spunky the spadefoot toad feels the need to move.

Emerging ever so slowly from his winter bed, he begins his journey away from the **uplands;** a higher point in the quiet Cape Cod woods.

On this rainy March evening with the dunes of the **Province Lands** behind them, Spunky is joined by hundreds of spadefoots.

The toads somehow sense that they must travel to a special damp place on the forest floor which is dry in summer, but fills with rain and melted snow from winter...

...a place called the **vernal pool**.

A seashore ranger is ready for the toads and has stopped a passing car so that the tiny creatures can get safely to the other side.

The ranger will close the road for as long as it takes the **endangered** spadefoots to complete their very important journey to the breeding grounds.

It is there that the spadefoot toad finds its mate once each year in the same spot, during the first rainy day of spring.

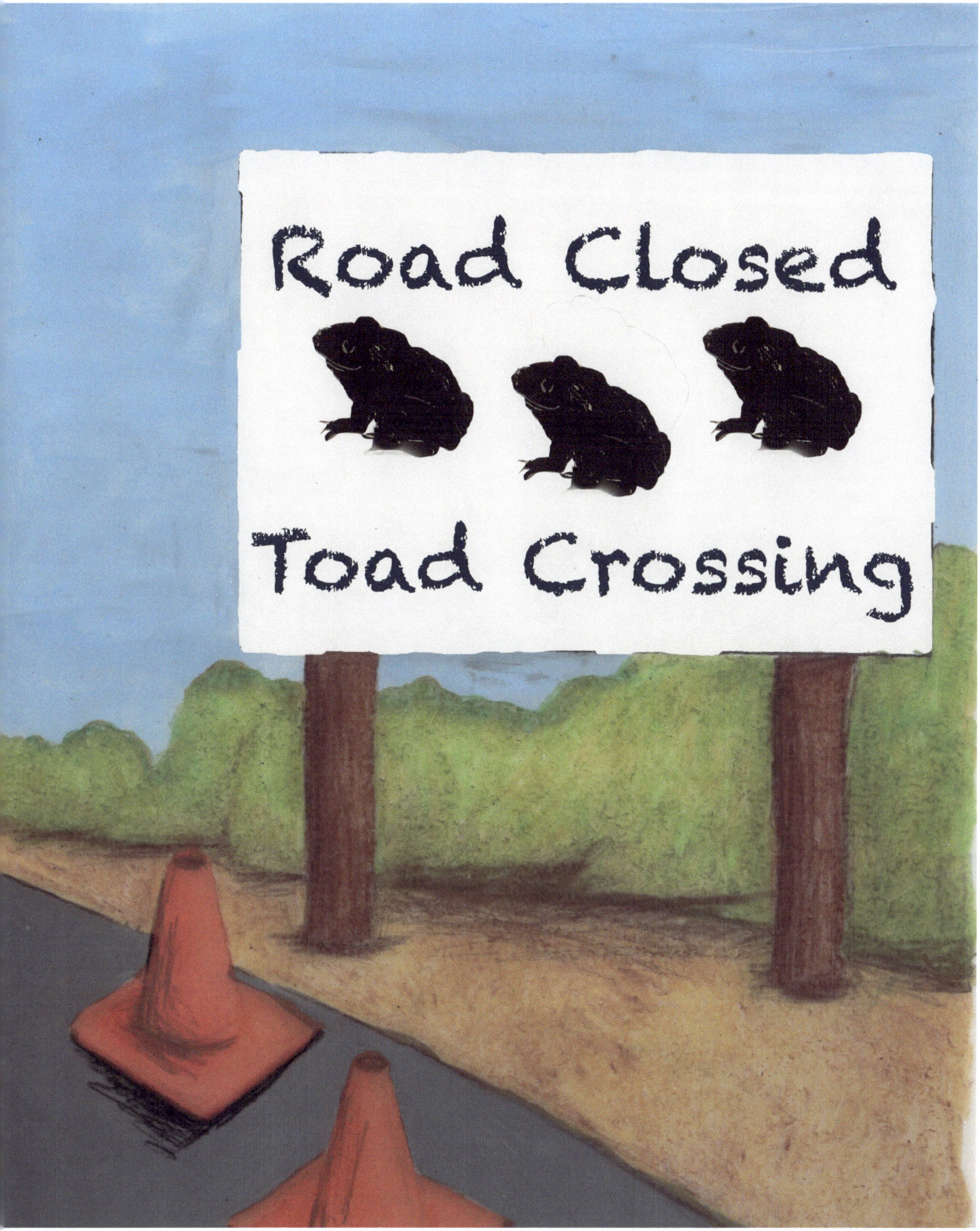
Road Closed
Toad Crossing

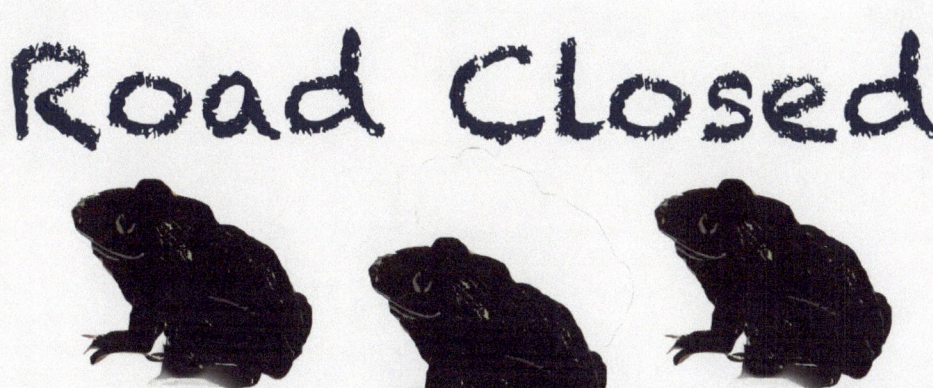

Peeking from a thick pile of rotting leaves, an **amphibian** with bright yellow dots prepares to join his spadefoot toad friends.

Elsewhere in the pool, graceful fairy shrimp spend their entire lives laying eggs that will hatch in early spring.

The adults can be seen darting excitedly in the quiet water, away from the **predators** which live in deeper waters, such as the **kettle ponds**.

By the time the warm summer sun has dried the water in the vernal pool, Spunky and his friends will have returned to the uplands...

Where Woody the wood frog will **forage** among the leaves along the forest floor and **hibernate** under moss, rocks, or rotting logs...

and Spunky the spadefoot toad
will use his specially-**adapted**
hind feet to dig himself a shelter
and await the next rainy spring
evening in March.

VERNAL POOL

Environmental Characteristics:

Permanently wet depressions in the Cape Cod landscape; fills with rain, melted water and run-off after spring snow or rain; usually dry by later summer. Does not support breeding populations of fish, which is good for other smaller life forms which could not survive permanent pond predators. These creatures must use a vernal pool for various parts of their life cycle.

Animal Life:

The Spring Peeper
The Yellow-Spotted Salamander
The Spadefoot Toad
The Mole Salamander
The Wood Frog
The Fairy Shrimp
(its presence means it is a genuine vernal pool)

VERNAL POOL GLOSSARY

Adaptation: a change in a plant or animal that makes it better able to live and survive in a particular place

Amphibian: a cold-blooded, smooth-skinned vertebrate

Endangered: a species at risk of disappearing from earth

Forage: to search for food

Hibernate: to sleep during winter

Kettle pond: a pond formed by the melting of glacial ice and replenished by rainwater

Predator: an organism that lives by preying on another organism

Province Lands: 3,500 acres of national parkland wilderness named in 1691 in Provincetown, Massachusetts

Upland: a high or hilly landscape

Vernal pool: a seasonal wetland that supports spring growth of certain specific species

THE AUTHOR

Heidi Clemmer was an educator at Wellfleet Elementary School for 21 years. Cape Cod Eco-Tales is the result of her passion for enlightening her students and others to the varied and significant eco-systems that dominate the Outer Cape landscape.

THE ILLUSTRATOR

Marisa Picariello is a Wellfleet resident who studied art at Wheaton College. She finds inspiration in the natural world and has always enjoyed exploring the Cape Cod landscape.